60

THE WORLD'S 60 BEST SKEWERS... PERIOD.
VÉRONIQUE PARADIS

PHOTOGRAPHER: Antoine Sicotte
ART DIRECTORS: Antoine Sicotte and Véronique Paradis
GRAPHIC DESIGNERS: Laurie Auger and Gabrielle Godbout
COVER DESIGNER: Laurie Auger
FOOD STYLIST: Véronique Paradis
ENGLISH TRANSLATOR: Lorien Jones
COPY EDITOR: Anna Phelan

PROJECT EDITOR: Antoine Ross Trempe

ISBN: 978-2-924155-14-1

Legal Deposit: 2014
Bibliothèque et Archives du Québec
Library and Archives Canada
ISBN : 978-2-924155-14-1

The publisher acknowledges the financial support of the Government of Canada through the Canada Book Fund (CBF) for its publishing activities and the support of the Government of Quebec through the tax credits for book publishing program (SODEC).

Originally published under the title *"Les 60 meilleures brochettes du monde... Point final."*

PRINTED IN CANADA

 Discover our upcoming books and much more!
WWW.FACEBOOK.COM/THEWORLDS60BEST

THE WORLD'S 60 BEST

SKEWERS

PERIOD.

THE WORLD'S 60 BEST

SKEWERS

PERIOD.

ABOUT THIS BOOK

The 60 skewers in this book are, in our opinion, the 60 best skewers in the world. Our team of chefs, writers, and foodies explored everything the culinary world has to offer to create this collection of the world's 60 best skewers.

We based our recipes on the following criteria:

QUALITY OF INGREDIENTS

ORIGINALITY

TASTE

APPEARANCE

SIMPLICITY

Are these our personal favorite skewers? Of course! But rest assured, our team of passionate, dedicated gourmets put time and loving care into formulating and testing each recipe in order to provide you with the 60 best skewers ever. In fact, our chef brought each freshly made skewer straight from the kitchen into the studio—no colorants, no sprays, no special effects added— and after each photo shoot, our creative team happily devoured the very skewers you see in these photos.

We hope you'll enjoy discovering these recipes and using this book as much as we enjoyed making it.

TABLE OF CONTENTS

INTRO

Every one of the 60 best recipes in this book features a flavor and cost legend (see pages 018 and 019) to guide your taste buds as well as your wallet in choosing the perfect dish. You will also find a glossary of culinary terms (page 029), handy cooking tips and tricks (page 025), and a list of must-have kitchen tools (page 023) that will help you create the world's BEST skewers. Finally, use the easy-to-follow Table of Contents (pages 010 and 011) and Ingredients Index (pages 176 to 181) to find everything you're looking for.

Impress guests with your food knowledge from our informative "Did you know?" sidebars, and take your meals to the next level thanks to our tasty tips and serving suggestions!

Bon appétit!

TIME

SPICY

RICH

COST

LEGEND

 PREPARATION TIME IN MINUTES, INCLUDING FREEZING TIME

HOT • PEPPERY • ZESTY

 LOW   MEDIUM   HIGH

CREAMY • BUTTERY • LUSCIOUS

 LOW   MEDIUM   HIGH

COST OF INGREDIENTS

 LOW   MEDIUM   HIGH

A SHORT HISTORY OF SKEWERS

The practice of cooking food on a stick has a history as old as humanity! Although it's difficult to directly trace its origins, we know that when our ancestors discovered fire, it was also necessary for them to develop a method of securing or suspending food above the open flame. The solution was to impale joints of meat or entire animals on a long, solid branch (essentially, a giant skewer), mount it on a spit, and turn it slowly over the heat, which allowed it to cook evenly and avoided the need to touch the hot food. Grilling food on skewers appears in Homer's ancient Greek epic poem The Odyssey, and excavations in Santorini, Greece uncovered firedogs, stone rests for skewers that are placed over a heat source, dating back to the 17th century BCE. It's said that during the Ottoman Empire, Turkish soldiers and wandering nomads would kill wild animals and use their swords and lances to roast meat over open fires. In Europe, roasting food on a spit reached the height of its popularity in the Middle Ages, when nearly every household had a spit in the kitchen fireplace, with a "spit boy" to rotate it by hand.

The spit was gradually replaced with smaller skewers. Naturally, the actual utensils are indispensible to cooking *en brochette*, as the French call it, and the type of skewer used depends on what's being cooked. Food is threaded onto, or pierced, with flat, round, or square skewers made of stainless steel, metal, wood, or bamboo, or even rosemary branches, sugarcane, or coconut palm fronds! Skewer sizes range from short and thin—ideal for piercing appetizers and bite-size snacks—to as long as 3 feet, like the long rods used for cooking Indian tandoori.

Because this method of cooking is so deep-rooted in our culinary history, virtually all cultures have their own version of food on a stick: there's the Middle Eastern *kebab*, now popular the world over, often served doner-style, where the meat is stacked horizontally on a vertical spit, roasted, and then carved; Greek *souvlaki*, which is meat, chicken, or pork usually served on a bed of rice, or in a pita with sauce; *satay*, one of Indonesia's national dishes, marinated with a spicy rub; and Japanese *yakitori*, traditionally served with *tare* sauce, made with mirin, sugar, soy sauce, and sake. And these are just the tip of the iceberg!

When most people think of skewers, they think of plain old marinated vegetables and chunks of meat or fish on the barbecue. But nowadays you can find anything and everything on a stick, from spaghetti and meatballs, to deep-fried chocolate bars, to mac and cheese, to scorpions and crickets! Food on a stick has become a street food specialty, and people flock in droves to stands and trucks, whether it's to nibble on exotic fare in a faraway place, or to sample the latest deep-fried fad at a summer fair. *The World's 60 Best Skewers... Period* offers the very best versions of classic and indigenous offerings, party-perfect appetizers, and creative new savory and sweet recipes. So toss the silverware and get skewering!

MUST-HAVE TOOLS

FOR THE WORLD'S BEST SKEWERS

1. A **barbecue** or a **grill pan with a ridged surface** for grilling your skewers

2. A **pastry** or **basting brush** for coating foods with delicious sauces and marinades

3. Metal and wooden **skewers**

4. A quality **pair of stainless steel tongs** for cooking your skewers like a pro

5. A **whisk** for emulsifying sauces, incorporating butter, and for whipping, beating, and mixing

6. A **hand blender** or a **food processor** for making pesto, chopping ingredients, and puréeing sauces and marinades without a hassle

7. A **mortar and pestle** for crushing, grinding, and mixing spices on the spot, to give your skewers the freshest flavor

8. A **large bowl** for preparing marinades and for marinating meat, fish, and more

9. **Resealable plastic bags** for quick and easy marinating, and to save space in the fridge

10. A **large pan** for cooking what needs to be cooked

11. A sharp **chef's knife** for chopping, cubing, dicing, slicing, and mincing

12. A **large pot** for blanching ingredients

13. A **mandoline** for thinly slicing and julienning quickly and precisely

14. A **zester** or **Microplane grater** for zesting citrus fruits

15. A **casserole dish** for cooking skewers in the oven

16. A **turning spatula** for flipping and manipulating fragile preparations

17. A **peeler** for peeling fruits and vegetables

TIPS & TRICKS

FOR CREATING THE WORLD'S BEST SKEWERS

1. If you're using the barbecue, it's very important to pre-soak your wooden skewers before cooking to prevent them from catching on fire or breaking. About 30 minutes in water should do the trick!

2. When assembling your skewers, spacing between ingredients is key. If they're too tightly packed the interiors will take too long to cook, while if they're spaced too far apart they'll quickly dry out.

3. We've created a multitude of versatile marinades and sauces that you can use for meats, fish, seafood, tofu... you name it! Consult the index at the back of the book for inspiration.

4. When a good price on meat presents itself and you buy it in bulk, marinate a large portion of it all at once and freeze it raw, along with the marinade. This is a great time saver, keeps the meat fresh, and won't break your wallet!

5. Use resealable plastic bags for marinating meat: just whip up your marinade of choice and toss it into the bag, along with the meat. Close the bag halfway, gently squeeze out all the excess air, and seal completely. Give it a little shake to coat the meat, and sit back and let the marinade work its magic.

6. To prevent ingredients from sticking to the cooking surface, oil the barbecue grill or grill pan, and not the skewers. It's much easier and you'll use much less oil.

7. You'll probably notice that most of the recipes in this book contain garlic. This extremely popular, aromatic bulb lends a deliciously earthy essence to savory dishes, but if you're not a fan, simply omit it from your recipe. Don't worry, it'll be just as tasty!

8. Feel free to use boneless chicken thighs instead of chicken breasts, if the recipe asks for chicken. The thighs are less expensive, and the darker meat is tender and full of flavor.

9. Skewers are perfect for entertaining: serve your guests mini brochettes as an appetizer, and heartier food on a stick as the main course. They're easily adaptable for vegetarian diets, and take just minutes to assemble, allowing you more time to spend with your friends and family.

10. Finally, always remember that the best skewers are made using the very freshest ingredients!

HOW-TO GUIDE

THE MEAT

Plenty of options exist when it comes to choosing cuts of meat for skewering. Because the meat is typically marinated, you don't necessarily need to use the tenderest cuts. The one type to avoid is stewing meat—because it requires a long cooking time to tenderize, it's much too tough for quick-cooking skewers.

Here are a few of our favorite cuts for skewers:

1. **CHICKEN:**   Boneless chicken breasts or thighs
2. **PORK:**   Pork tenderloin or pork shoulder, if it's marinated long enough
3. **LAMB:**   Boneless saddle or leg of lamb
4. **BEEF:**   Sirloin or tenderloin

THE MARINADE

Marinade is an essential element of scrumptious skewers, tenderizing the meat, rendering it succulent and juicy, and infusing it with oodles of flavor.

Most marinades are composed of three basic ingredients: a fat, an acid, and flavorings.

- The acidic content in the marinade, usually citrus, wine, or vinegar, is what softens the meat by breaking down the tough connective tissue.

- The oil in a marinade, whether it's oil, yogurt, coconut milk, or cream, prevents the meat from drying out, and will give it a lovely color and help it grill up beautifully.

- The flavorings—that is, the spices, herbs, garlic, or onion—are what provide a marinade's unique flavor.

The marinating time will vary depending on the meat (or seafood or meat alternative) you're using. The longer food marinates, the more tender it will be, but delicate ingredients, such as fish and seafood with its loose, soft tissue, shouldn't be left to marinate for too long—the acid in the marinade will actually start to cook it. If you're marinating fish and seafood, keep an eye on the sides and surface of the food; if it starts becoming slightly opaque, it's time to take it out of the marinade.

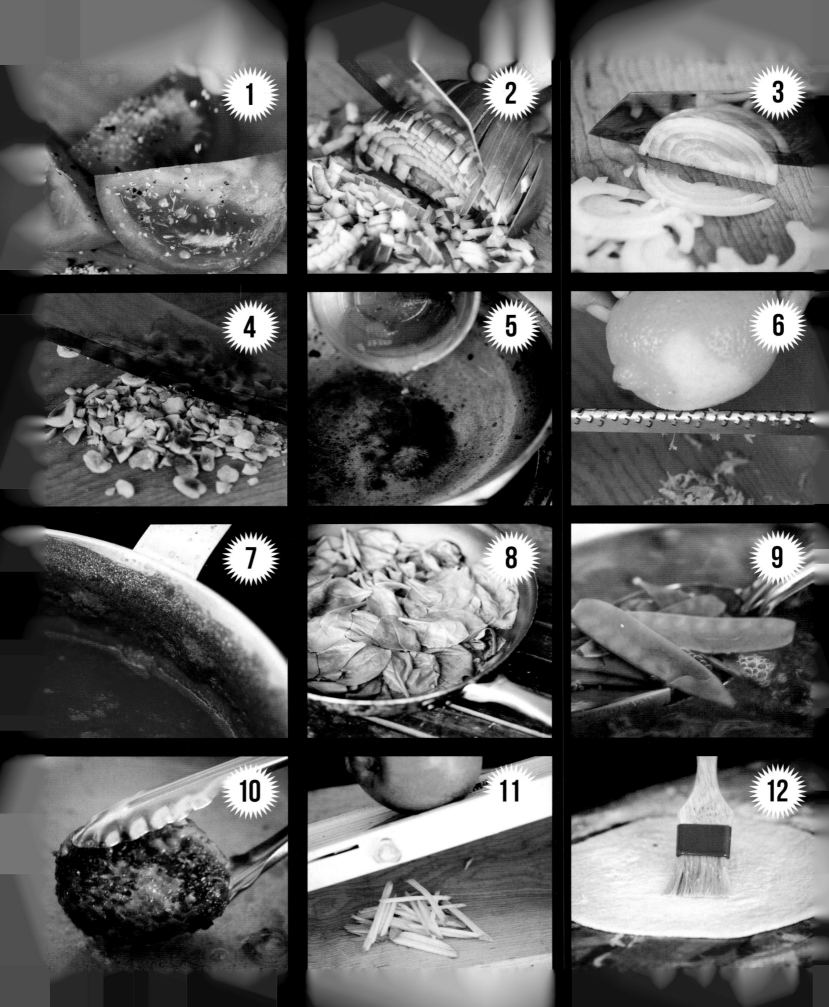

GLOSSARY

1. SEASON

To improve the flavor of a dish by adding salt and pepper to taste.

2. DICE

A basic knife cut in which food is cut into cubes.

3. THINLY SLICE

To cut into thin, equal slices.

4. CHOP

To cut into small pieces with a sharp instrument (knife or food processor).

5. DEGLAZE

To remove and dissolve caramelized bits of food at the bottom of a pan in order to make a jus or sauce.

6. ZEST

To remove the zest, or outer skin, of citrus fruits with a zester, Microplane grater, or peeling knife.

7. REDUCE

To thicken a liquid by evaporating over heat.

8. WILT

To cook certain vegetables (spinach, Swiss chard, kale, sorrel, etc.) over low heat, with or without a fat, in order to reduce their volume and release some of their liquid.

9. BLANCH

To cook vegetables briefly in boiling salted water.

10. SEAR

To cook in fat (butter or oil) at a high temperature to obtain a golden or brown crust.

11. JULIENNE

A basic knife cut in which food is cut into long, thin strips. A mandoline is often used for this cut.

12. BRUSH

To coat a food surface with a thin layer of liquid or sauce using a brush or the back of a spoon.

THE CHEF'S SECRET

Every seasoned chef will attest that the real secret to creating a successful dish is to *taste! taste! taste!* Taste before and after seasoning, add some heat or a squeeze of lemon juice if you think your dish needs a little kick, or go ahead and double the herbs or even the cheese! The most important thing is to follow your instincts and your senses. Listen for that telltale sizzle, inhale the tantalizing aromas, and CONSTANTLY taste your food so you can get to know your dish in all its stages.

There you have it—the simple secret to creating delicious, original dishes.

PIRI-PIRI QUAIL

4 SKEWERS

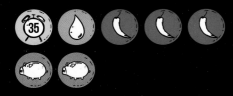

MARINATING TIME: 4 HOURS

8 quails

FOR PIRI-PIRI MARINADE

1/2 cup (125 ml) piri-piri sauce
1 onion, halved
4 cloves garlic
Juice of 2 lemons
1 cup (250 ml) pale ale
1 tbsp sugar
1 tsp salt
1/3 cup (80 ml) vegetable oil

PREPARATION

With a hand blender, or in a food processor, purée all marinade ingredients.

With a large, sharp knife, split each bird in half by cutting along the spine.

Arrange quails in a large dish or container. Pour marinade over top and mix well, making sure the birds are completely coated. Let marinate in the refrigerator for at least 4 hours.

Thread 4 quail halves lengthwise onto each skewer.

Transfer marinade to a small pot and let reduce until it turns into a thick sauce.

Grill quails over medium heat on the barbecue for 20 minutes, turning halfway through cooking and brushing with sauce every 5 minutes. Serve with roasted potatoes and a crisp green salad.

 DID YOU KNOW?

Piri-piri sauce is a spicy and fragrant Portuguese chili sauce that is commonly used as a marinade for the famously fiery *frango grelhado com piri-piri*, or grilled chicken with piri-piri sauce.

2

NIPPON TUNA

8 SKEWERS

MARINATING TIME: 30 MINUTES

 **DID YOU KNOW?**

The Atlantic Bluefin tuna can grow up to 15 feet long, and weigh up to 1,500 lbs. In the wild, some species of tuna are known to live anywhere from 15 to 30 years!

FOR TUNA

1 lb (16 oz) fresh white or red tuna, cut into 1-1/2-inch cubes
1 tbsp vegetable oil
1 tbsp black and white sesame seeds

FOR ASIAN-STYLE MARINADE

1/2 cup (125 ml) soy sauce
1/4 cup (60 ml) mirin
1 clove garlic, chopped
1 inch fresh ginger, peeled and chopped

PREPARATION

In a bowl, combine all marinade ingredients. Add cubed tuna, mix well, and let marinate for at least 30 minutes, but no longer than 2 hours.

Remove tuna from marinade and thread onto pre-soaked wooden skewers. Reserve marinade.

In a large pan, heat oil over high heat and sear tuna for about 10 to 15 seconds on each side. Transfer skewers to a plate, add reserved marinade to pan, and reduce until it turns into a syrupy sauce. Serve tuna skewers over a bed of cucumber salad. Drizzle sauce over all and sprinkle with sesame seeds.

BEEF WITH RED WINE & HERBS

4 SKEWERS

MARINATING TIME: 4 HOURS

INGREDIENTS

1 lb (16 oz) beef, cut into 1-inch cubes
12 button mushrooms, stems removed
1 onion, cut into 1-inch squares
1 red pepper, seeded and cut into 1-inch squares
1 orange pepper, seeded and cut into 1-inch squares

FOR RED WINE MARINADE

1/2 cup (125 ml) red wine
2 tsp *herbes de Provence*
2 tbsp balsamic vinegar
1/4 cup (60 ml) olive oil
3 cloves garlic, chopped
1 tsp black pepper, cracked

PREPARATION

In a bowl, combine all marinade ingredients. Add beef cubes, mix well, and let marinate in the refrigerator for at least 4 hours.

Alternate cubed beef with the onion, red pepper, and orange pepper on 4 oiled wooden skewers.

Grill skewers over high heat on the barbecue, or in a grill pan with a ridged surface, for 5 to 10 minutes until beef reaches the desired doneness, turning halfway through cooking.

Serve with prepared pepper or mushroom demi-glace, if desired.

ITALIAN NIBBLES

12 SKEWERS

 **DID YOU KNOW?**

The Italian word *bocconcini* means "small mouthfuls," a fitting name for these cheeses, about the size, color, and shape of an egg. Because of their appearance, and because they were once only made with the milk of water buffaloes, they're also sometimes called *uova di bufala*, or "buffalo eggs".

FOR POLENTA

2 cups (500 ml) water
1/2 cup (125 ml) cornmeal (polenta)
1 cup (250 ml) Gruyere cheese, grated
Salt and freshly ground pepper
1 tbsp butter

FOR SKEWERS

12 mini bocconcini
1 tsp white balsamic vinegar
1 tbsp olive oil
12 stuffed olives of your choice
12 cherry tomatoes
12 fresh basil leaves

PREPARATION

In a pot, bring water to a boil. Gradually sprinkle in cornmeal, whisking constantly to prevent lumps from forming. Cook, stirring, for 3 to 4 minutes over low heat. Remove from heat, stir in cheese, and season with salt and pepper. Mix well.

Line a baking sheet with plastic wrap. Pour hot polenta over top and spread out into an even, 1-inch-thick layer. Cover polenta with another piece of plastic wrap and refrigerate for 30 minutes, or until polenta is cool and has completely set.

In a bowl, combine mini bocconcini, balsamic vinegar, and olive oil.

Thread 1 olive, 1 tomato, 1 basil leaf, and 1 mini bocconcini onto each skewer.

Slice chilled polenta into 1-1/2-inch squares. In a non-stick pan, melt butter and fry polenta cubes until golden. Serve each skewer on a warm polenta cube.

SHRIMP & PAPRIKA PARTY

4 SKEWERS

MARINATING TIME: 1 HOUR

FOR SKEWERS

20 medium pre-shelled shrimp
2 tbsp fresh cilantro, chopped
1 lime, cut into wedges

FOR LIME & PAPRIKA MARINADE

1/2 tsp smoked paprika
1 tsp mild paprika
1/4 cup (60 ml) vegetable oil
Juice of 1 lime
1 tbsp brown sugar
1/4 tsp salt
1/4 tsp freshly ground pepper

PREPARATION

In a bowl, combine all marinade ingredients. Add shrimp, mix well, and let marinate in the refrigerator for at least 1 hour.

Thread shrimp onto pre-soaked wooden skewers.

Grill skewers over high heat on the barbecue, or in a grill pan with a ridged surface, for 3 to 4 minutes, turning halfway through cooking. Sprinkle with fresh cilantro and serve with lime wedges.

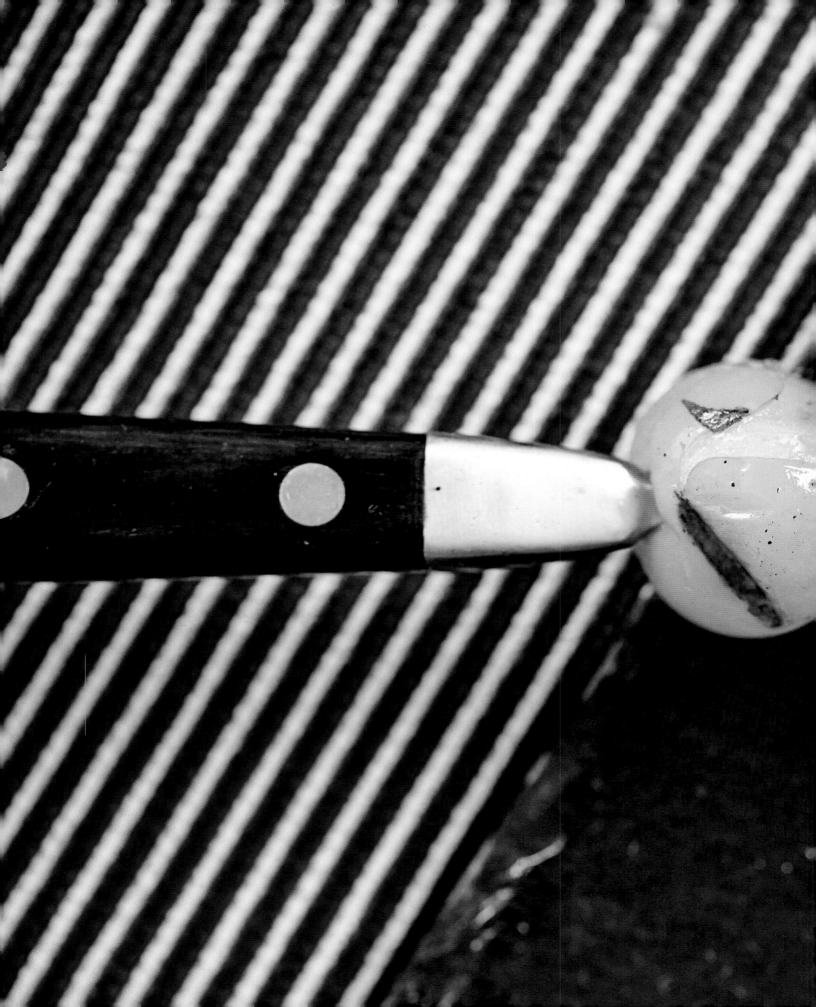

6

GRILLED HALLOUMI

6 SKEWERS

INGREDIENTS

1/2 lb (8 oz) halloumi cheese, cut into 1-inch cubes
1 small eggplant, cut into 1-1/2-inch cubes
18 yellow cherry tomatoes
1 red pepper, cut into 1-inch squares
1 red onion, cut into 1-inch squares
1 yellow pepper, cut into 1-inch squares
1 tbsp dried oregano
1/4 cup (60 ml) olive oil
2 tbsp balsamic vinegar
Salt and freshly ground pepper

PREPARATION

Rinse halloumi under cold water for 2 minutes to remove excess salt.

In a large bowl, combine all ingredients and mix well.

Alternately thread ingredients onto pre-soaked wooden skewers.

Grill skewers over medium heat on the barbecue, or in a grill pan with a ridged surface, for 10 to 12 minutes, turning halfway through cooking. Serve as a side dish, or double the recipe and serve as a main course, over a bed of spinach.

DID YOU KNOW?

Semi-soft, salty halloumi has a higher melting point than most cheeses, which makes it an ideal cheese for frying and grilling.

CHICKEN SOUVLAKI

6 SKEWERS

MARINATING TIME: 6 HOURS

2 chicken breasts, cut into 1-inch cubes

FOR SOUVLAKI MARINADE

Juice and zest of 2 lemons
1/4 cup (60 ml) fresh oregano, chopped
2 cloves garlic, chopped
1/3 cup (80 ml) olive oil
Salt and freshly ground pepper

PREPARATION

In a large bowl, combine all marinade ingredients. Add chicken and mix well. Cover and let marinate in the refrigerator for at least 6 hours.

Thread chicken onto pre-soaked wooden skewers.

Grill skewers over medium heat on the barbecue for 10 to 12 minutes, turning a few times during cooking. Serve with Greek salad, or pita bread and tzatziki.

 DID YOU KNOW?

In some regions of Greece, *souvlaki* is the name of a popular pita sandwich stuffed with meat that has been grilled on skewers, while the meat skewers themselves are called *kalamaki* (little reed).

SPICED BEEF KEBABS

8 SKEWERS

INGREDIENTS

1 tsp olive oil
1 onion, finely chopped
1 tbsp tomato paste
1 tsp cinnamon
1/2 tsp cumin
1/2 tsp mild paprika
1/2 tsp crushed red pepper flakes
1 lb (16 oz) ground beef
1/4 cup (60 ml) fresh cilantro, chopped
Salt and freshly ground pepper
2 tbsp vegetable oil

PREPARATION

In a pan, heat oil and sauté onion for 1 minute. Add tomato paste and spices and cook for 2 to 3 minutes longer. Remove from heat and let sit for 5 minutes.

In a bowl, combine onion and spices with ground beef. Add cilantro and mix well. Season generously with salt and pepper.

Gently pack meat mixture around pre-soaked wooden skewers.

Brush skewers with a bit of oil and transfer to a baking sheet. Cook in a 400°F (200°C) oven for 15 minutes, or on the barbecue on top of a sheet of aluminum foil, turning a few times during cooking. Serve with a spicy tomato sauce or hummus.

TERIYAKI SALMON

4 SKEWERS

FOR SKEWERS

1 lb (16 oz) salmon, cut into 1-1/2-inch cubes
Vegetables of your choice (zucchini, bell pepper, onion, asparagus, tomato, mushrooms, etc.), cut into 1-inch pieces

FOR TERIYAKI SAUCE

1/4 cup (60 ml) soy sauce
1/4 cup (60 ml) mirin
2 tbsp brown sugar
1 clove garlic, chopped
1 tsp cornstarch
2 tbsp water

PREPARATION

In a small pot, bring soy sauce, mirin, brown sugar, and garlic to a boil. Let simmer for 2 minutes. Dilute cornstarch in water and add to sauce. Stir and let simmer for 1 minute. Remove from heat and let cool completely before using.

In a bowl, combine 1/4 cup (60 ml) cooled teriyaki sauce with cubed salmon.

Alternately thread salmon and vegetables onto pre-soaked wooden skewers.

Brush skewers generously with teriyaki sauce and grill over high heat for 5 to 6 minutes on the barbecue, or in a grill pan with a ridged surface, turning and brushing with more sauce a few times during cooking. Serve.

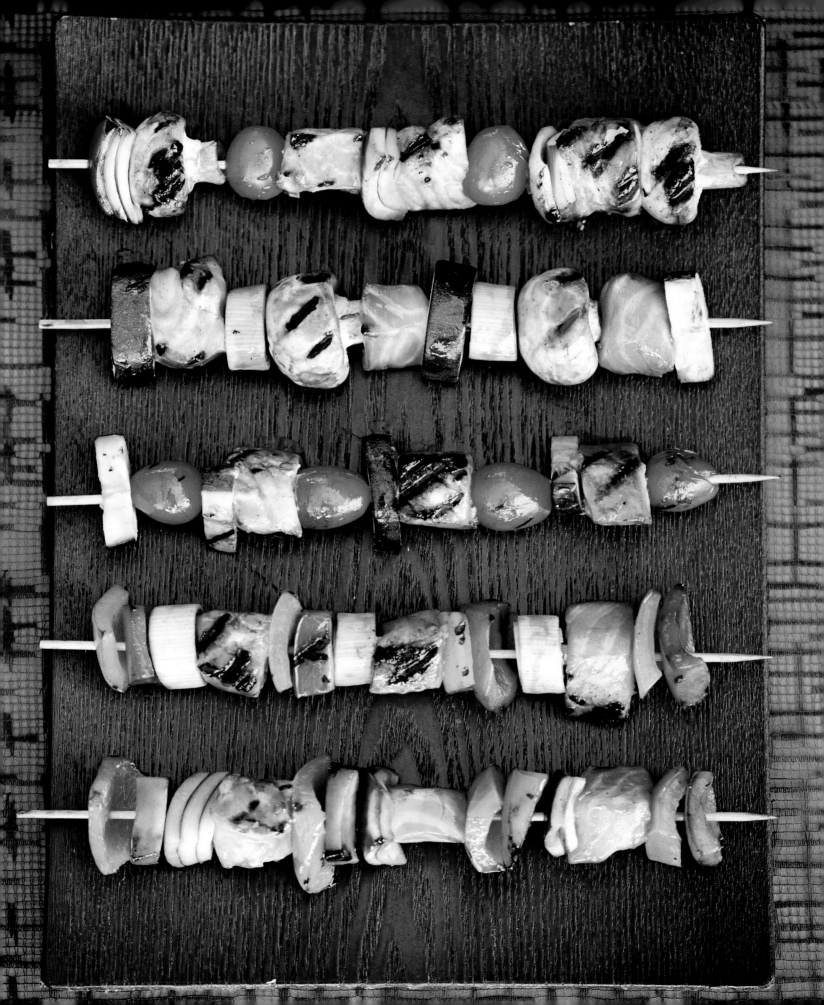

10

LAMB CHOPS & GRAPE VINE BUNDLES

4 SKEWERS

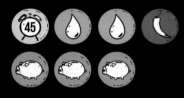

MARINATING TIME: 4 HOURS

 **DID YOU KNOW?**

After the Renaissance, many paintings and sculptures depicting nudity were judged to be indecent. Vine leaves were added to many classic works of art to cover the "offensive" parts.

FOR SKEWERS

8 lamb chops
8 grape vine leaves
8 pieces feta cheese, cut into 2-inch-long sticks
2 tbsp sugar
1 lemon, quartered

FOR PORK CHOP MARINADE

Juice and zest of 1 lemon
8 cloves garlic, chopped
1 tsp peppercorns, cracked
1/4 tsp salt
2 tbsp fresh rosemary, chopped
1/3 cup (80 ml) olive oil

PREPARATION

In a bowl, combine all marinade ingredients. Add lamb chops and mix well to fully coat. Transfer to a casserole dish and let marinate in the refrigerator for at least 4 hours.

Bring a large pot of water to a boil and blanch grape vine leaves for 5 minutes. Drain and very gently pat dry.

On a flat work surface, lay out a grape vine leaf with the stem pointing towards you. Cut off the stem and place a stick of feta horizontally just above the base of the leaf. Fold the stem end of the leaf up over the feta. Fold in the 2 sides towards the center and roll up as tightly as possible towards the top of the leaf. Repeat with remaining vine leaves and feta. Transfer vine leaf bundles to the casserole dish with the lamb, coat with marinade, and let marinate for at least 2 hours.

Pre-soak 8 wooden skewers. Alternately thread 2 lamb chops and 2 grape vine bundles onto 2 skewers, so the sides lie flat on the grill. Repeat with remaining chops and grape vine bundles.

Pour sugar onto a small plate and coat lemons in sugar (leave peel uncoated). Thread a wedge of lemon onto the end of each skewer and grill over medium heat on the barbecue for 5 to 7 minutes on each side, until lamb is cooked to desired doneness. Serve.

FIERY BEEF & BELL PEPPER

4 SKEWERS

MARINATING TIME: 2 HOURS

FOR SKEWERS

1 lb (16 oz) beef, cut into 1-inch cubes
1 red pepper, cut into 1-1/2-inch squares
1 orange pepper, cut into 1-1/2-inch squares
1 yellow pepper, cut into 1-1/2-inch squares
1 onion, cut into 1-1/2-inch squares
2 tbsp vegetable oil
Salt and freshly ground pepper

FOR RED CURRY & COCONUT MARINADE

2 tbsp red curry paste
2 tbsp soy sauce
1 tsp sesame oil
1/4 cup (60 ml) coconut milk
2 tbsp vegetable oil

PREPARATION

In a large bowl, combine beef cubes with all marinade ingredients. Let marinate in the refrigerator for at least 2 hours.

In another bowl, combine vegetables and vegetable oil. Season with salt and pepper.

Alternately thread beef and vegetables onto oiled skewers.

Grill over high heat on the barbecue, or in a grill pan with a ridged surface, for 6 to 10 minutes, until beef is cooked to desired doneness. Serve over a bed of rice.

 DID YOU KNOW?

Thai curries differ from Indian curries, in that they're made with a paste of fresh ingredients (like herbs, garlic, and lemongrass) combined with spices, instead of just a mix of dried spices.

BRUNCH BROCHETTES

4 SKEWERS

FOR SKEWERS

1 tbsp butter
24 cubes country bread, 1-1/2 inches x 1-1/2 inches each
24 fresh raspberries
24 large, fresh blueberries

FOR FRENCH TOAST BATTER

1/3 cup (80 ml) milk
2 tbsp brown sugar
2 eggs
1/4 tsp vanilla extract
1/4 tsp cinnamon

PREPARATION

In a large bowl, whisk together all French toast batter ingredients.

In a large non-stick pan, melt butter. Add bread cubes to French toast batter and mix to coat, so that the bread absorbs the batter. Quickly drain using a wire mesh strainer to remove any excess batter. Transfer to the pan and cook for 1 to 2 minutes on each side, until golden brown all over.

Alternately thread French toast cubes, raspberries, and blueberries onto pre-soaked wooden skewers.

Warm skewers for a few minutes in the oven and serve doused with maple syrup.

 **DID YOU KNOW?**

In France, French toast is actually called *pain perdu*, meaning "lost" (or "wasted") bread, as it was traditionally made to use up bread that had gone stale.

SUNDRIED TOMATO CHICKEN SKEWERS

6 SKEWERS

MARINATING TIME: 4 HOURS

6 boneless, skinless chicken thighs, cut into 1-inch cubes

FOR SUNDRIED TOMATO MARINADE

1/4 cup (60 ml) white wine
8 sundried tomatoes
1 tbsp balsamic vinegar
1 clove garlic
2 tbsp fresh Parmesan cheese, grated
1/4 cup (60 ml) olive oil
2 tbsp almond flour or whole toasted almonds
8 fresh basil leaves
Salt and freshly ground pepper

PREPARATION

In a food processor, purée all marinade ingredients until smooth. In a bowl, combine marinade and chicken cubes. Cover and let marinate in the refrigerator for at least 4 hours.

Preheat oven to 400°F (200°C).

Thread chicken onto oiled skewers. Place on a baking sheet lined with parchment paper and cook for 15 minutes in the oven. Serve with rice and grilled vegetables.

BEEF & CHIMICHURRI

4 SKEWERS

 **TASTY TIP**

If you're pressed for time, or have last-minute guests stopping by, you can always pick up a pre-marinated beef tenderloin; just make sure the marinade pairs well with chimichurri sauce.

 DID YOU KNOW?

Chimichurri is also used as a marinade for grilled meats.

FOR SKEWERS

1 lb (16 oz) skirt steak
Salt and freshly ground pepper
2 tbsp cornstarch
Vegetable oil for frying

FOR CHIMICHURRI SAUCE

1-1/2 cups (375 ml) fresh parsley, with stems
2 cloves garlic
1/4 cup (60 ml) fresh oregano
1 tsp paprika
1/2 cup (125 ml) olive oil
2 tbsp red (or white) wine vinegar
Salt and freshly ground pepper
1 tsp crushed red pepper flakes

PREPARATION

With a hand blender, or in a food processor, purée chimichurri ingredients until smooth. Let sit for 30 minutes.

Slice beef into long strips, cutting against the grain.

Thread beef strips onto pre-soaked wooden skewers. Season generously with salt and pepper, and then coat with cornstarch.

In a large pot, heat 1-1/2 inches of vegetable oil. When oil is hot, fry brochettes for 2 to 3 minutes, until meat is lightly browned. Remove with tongs and drain on paper towels. Serve with chimichurri sauce for dipping.

SWEET & SOUR JUMBO SHRIMP

12 SKEWERS

MARINATING TIME: 30 MINUTES

FOR SKEWERS

12 jumbo shrimp, peeled and deveined, tails left on
1 tbsp vegetable oil

FOR SWEET & SOUR SAUCE

1/4 cup (60 ml) rice vinegar
1/4 cup (60 ml) sugar
1/4 cup (60 ml) tomato paste
1 tbsp soy sauce
2 cloves garlic, chopped
1/2 inch fresh ginger, peeled and chopped
2 green onions, thinly sliced

PREPARATION

In a bowl, whisk together all sauce ingredients.

Using a small paring knife, make 4 or 5 cuts along the inside of each shrimp, to make them easier to skewer vertically. Thread shrimp onto pre-soaked skewers, starting with the tails. Brush generously with sauce.

Transfer to a dish, cover, and let marinate in the refrigerator for at least 30 minutes.

Grill for 4 to 5 minutes on the barbecue over high heat, turning and brushing with sauce halfway through. Or, fry in a pan in vegetable oil, adding a bit of sauce near the end of cooking to coat and keep shrimp tender and juicy. Serve.

CHORIZO & CRISPY, MELTY MOZZA

4 SKEWERS

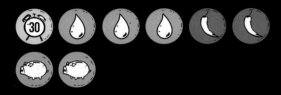

INGREDIENTS

8 cubes smoked mozzarella cheese (caciocavallo),
1 inch x 1 inch each
2 tbsp flour
1 egg, beaten
1/2 cup (125 ml) Italian breadcrumbs
4 mini sweet peppers
1/2 radicchio, cut into 8 pieces
8 chorizo sausage rounds, 1/2 inch thick each
2 tbsp vegetable oil

FOR VINAIGRETTE

1/4 cup (60 ml) olive oil
2 tbsp balsamic vinegar

PREPARATION

Dredge cheese cubes in flour, dip in egg, and coat with bread-crumbs. Gently press in breadcrumbs to make sure they stick. Dip in egg and coat with breadcrumbs a second time. Set aside.

Thread a mini pepper onto each skewer, and then alternately add radicchio, mozzarella, and chorizo rounds.

In a large non-stick pan, heat vegetable oil and cook skewers for 1 to 2 minutes on each side, or until cheese is beautifully golden on all sides.

In a small bowl, whisk together olive oil and balsamic vinegar. Drizzle over skewers, avoiding the cheese cubes, right before serving.

DID YOU KNOW?

Like the endive, wine-red radicchio is a type of chicory; it has a bold flavor and pleasing bitterness that mellows with cooking.

17

LAMB KOFTA & SPICY SOUR CREAM SAUCE

12 SKEWERS

FOR LAMB KOFTA

1 tbsp cumin seeds, crushed
1 tbsp coriander seeds, crushed
1 tbsp fennel seeds, crushed
1 tsp crushed red pepper flakes
2 tbsp olive oil
1 shallot, finely chopped
2 cloves garlic, chopped
1 lb (16 oz) ground lamb
1 egg
1/4 cup (60 ml) breadcrumbs
Salt and freshly ground pepper

FOR SPICY SOUR CREAM SAUCE

1/2 cup (125 ml) sour cream
1 tsp harissa
1 store-bought roasted red pepper, chopped
2 tbsp fresh cilantro, chopped
Salt and freshly ground pepper

PREPARATION

In a small bowl, combine cumin seeds, coriander seeds, fennel seeds, and crushed red pepper flakes.

In a small pan, heat olive oil and sauté shallot and garlic for 1 minute. Add spices and cook for 1 minute longer.

In a large bowl, combine ground lamb, egg, breadcrumbs, and the onion, garlic, and spice mixture. Mix well and season with salt and pepper. Gently pack meat mixture around pre-soaked wooden skewers. Place on a baking sheet and cook in a 400°F (200°F) oven for 20 minutes, or on the barbecue for 20 minutes over medium heat.

In a small bowl, combine sour cream, harissa, roasted red pepper, and cilantro. Season with salt and pepper and serve with kofta.

18

MONKFISH PROVENÇAL

4 SKEWERS

FOR SKEWERS

1/2 lb (8 oz) monkfish fillet
2 Italian tomatoes, cut into 4
1/2 bulb fennel, cut into cubes
4 slices bacon, cut into 1-1/2-inch pieces

FOR PROVENÇAL MARINADE

1 tbsp capers
2 anchovies
2 tbsp fresh parsley
2 shallots
Juice of 1 lemon
1/4 tsp freshly ground pepper

PREPARATION

In a food processor, purée all marinade ingredients.

If necessary, remove the monkfish fillet's center bone by running a knife very closely down the side of the backbone. Repeat on the other side of the spine to completely detach the bone and obtain 2 smaller fillets. Cut fish into 1-inch cubes and combine with tomatoes, fennel, and marinade.

Alternately thread monkfish, tomatoes, bacon, and fennel onto pre-soaked wooden skewers.

Grill over medium heat for 10 minutes on the barbecue, or in a grill pan with a ridged surface, turning halfway through cooking. Serve with salad.

DID YOU KNOW?

Fishmongers almost never sell whole monkfish for one very obvious reason: it's extremely ugly, and nobody would buy it! In fact, in the past, before it became a popular cooking fish, fishermen would simply throw it back into the water; it was believed that monkfish were monsters that would bring bad luck..

19

THE BIG BBQ CHICKEN & BACON

6 SKEWERS

MARINATING TIME: 1 HOUR

DID YOU KNOW?

The original recipe for HP Sauce was invented by Frederick Gibson Garton, a grocer from Nottingham, England. The famous condiment inherited the initials "HP" when its creator heard that a restaurant in the British Houses of Parliament was serving it!

FOR SKEWERS

2 chicken breasts, cut into 1-1/2-inch cubes
18 button mushrooms
4 slices bacon, cut into 4
1 red onion, cut into 1-1/2-inch squares

FOR BARBECUE MARINADE

1 clove garlic, chopped
1/2 cup (125 ml) ketchup
1 tbsp Worcestershire sauce
1 tbsp HP Sauce
1/4 cup (60 ml) brown sugar
2 tbsp vegetable oil
1 tsp steak spice

PREPARATION

In a bowl, combine all marinade ingredients. Add chicken and mushrooms, mix well to coat, and let marinate in the refrigerator for at least 1 hour.

Alternately thread chicken, bacon, onion, and mushrooms onto pre-soaked wooden skewers.

Grill over medium heat for 12 to 15 minutes on the barbecue, or in a grill pan with ridged surface, brushing skewers with marinade and turning them 2 or 3 times during cooking. Serve.

MELON FETA TOWERS

6 SKEWERS

INGREDIENTS

18 squares watermelon, 1 inch x 1 inch each
12 squares feta cheese, 1 inch x 1 inch each
2 tbsp fresh mint, chopped
1/2 tsp Espelette pepper
1 tsp white balsamic vinegar
1 tbsp grapeseed oil

PREPARATION

Alternately thread 3 squares watermelon and 2 squares feta cheese onto each skewer.

In a small bowl, combine mint, Espelette pepper, balsamic vinegar, and oil. Drizzle a bit of the mixture over each skewer and serve.

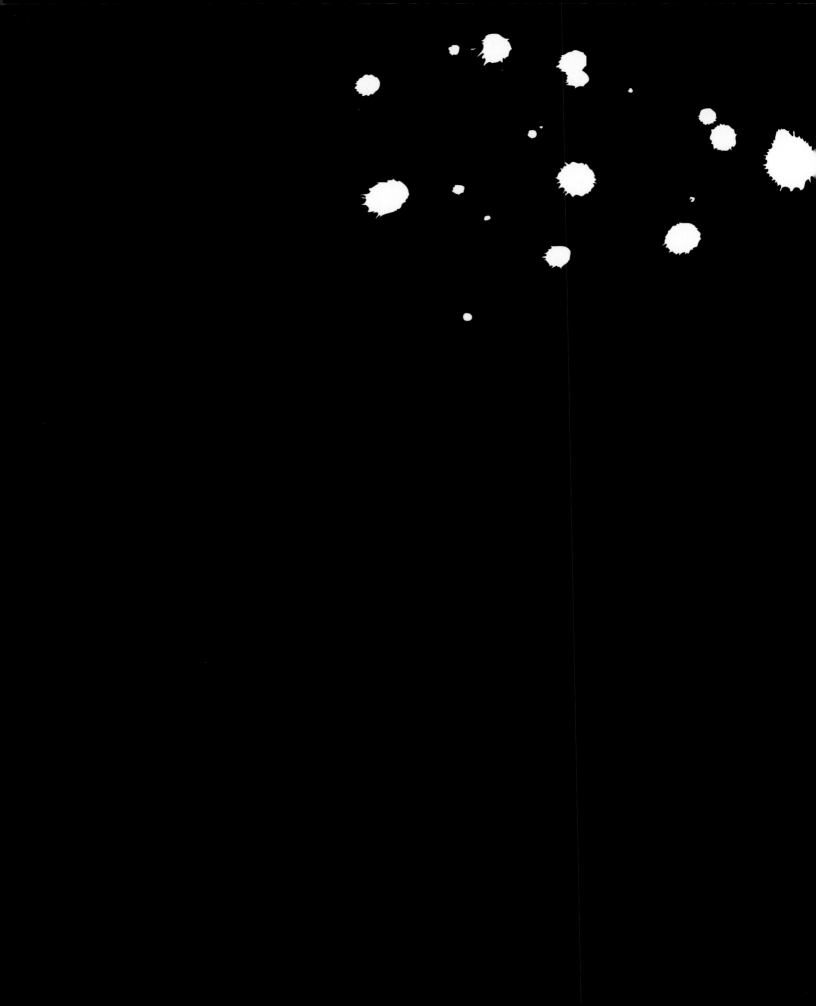

LAMB BITES & GOAT CHEESE SAUCE

15 SKEWERS

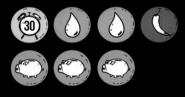

MARINATING TIME: 4 HOURS

TASTY TIP

For extra freshness, add a small handful of chopped mint leaves to your goat cheese dip.

DID YOU KNOW?

Garam masala is a popular Indian blend of toasted ground spices, usually comprising cinnamon, cardamom, cumin, cloves, black pepper, and bay leaf, although mixtures vary regionally.

1 lb (16 oz) boneless leg of lamb

FOR MASALA MARINADE

1 tbsp garam masala
1 tbsp tomato paste
1/4 cup (60 ml) olive oil
1/4 cup (60 ml) white wine
2 tbsp fresh parsley, chopped
Salt and freshly ground pepper

FOR GOAT CHEESE SAUCE

1 cup (250 ml) plain yogurt
1/4 cup (60 ml) fresh goat cheese
1 tsp Espelette pepper
2 tbsp olive oil
1 clove garlic, chopped
1/2 tsp salt
1/2 tsp freshly ground black pepper

PREPARATION

Cut lamb into bite-size pieces, slicing against the grain of the meat (if you slice with the grain, you'll end up with tough, stringy pieces).

In a bowl, combine all marinade ingredients. Add lamb, mix well, and let marinate in the refrigerator for at least 4 hours.

With a hand blender, purée goat cheese sauce ingredients until nice and creamy. Set aside.

Thread lamb pieces onto the ends of pre-soaked wooden skewers. On the barbecue over high heat, grill skewers for 3 to 4 minutes on each side. Serve with goat cheese sauce for dipping.

TOFU INFERNO!

8 SKEWERS

MARINATING TIME: 2 HOURS

FOR SKEWERS

1/2 lb (8 oz) firm tofu, cut into 1-inch cubes
1 red pepper, seeded and cut i squares
1 yellow pepper, seeded and cut into squares
1 zucchini, cut in half lengthwise and sliced into half-moons
1 leek, sliced into rounds

FOR SPICY ASIAN MARINADE

2 tbsp sriracha
1 tbsp honey
1/4 cup (60 ml) soy sauce
1 tsp sesame oil
2 tbsp vegetable oil
Salt and freshly ground pepper

PREPARATION

In a bowl, combine all marinade ingredients. Add tofu and mix well. Cover and let marinate in the refrigerator for at least 2 hours.

Add vegetables to tofu and marinade and toss well to coat. Alternately thread tofu and vegetables onto pre-soaked wooden skewers.

Grill over medium heat on the barbecue, or in a grill pan with a ridged surface, for 8 to 10 minutes, turning them a few times during cooking. When vegetables are fully cooked through, remove from heat and serve.

 **DID YOU KNOW?**

Tofu will keep for 7 to 10 days in water in the refrigerator, so long as the water is changed every day.

BEEF SURPRISE SKEWERS

8 SKEWERS

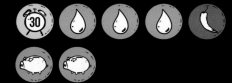

MARINATING TIME: 15 MINUTES

FOR SKEWERS

16 slices Chinese fondue (hot pot) beef (very thinly sliced beef for dipping)
8 pieces cheddar cheese, cut into 1-1/2-inch x 1/4-inch sticks

FOR RED WINE & SOY MARINADE

1/4 cup (60 ml) red wine
1/4 cup (60 ml) beef stock
2 tbsp olive oil
1 tbsp sugar
1 tbsp soy sauce
1 tsp dried oregano

PREPARATION

On a flat work surface, lay out 2 slices of beef, slightly overlapping. Place a pre-soaked wooden skewer on top of the beef, and then a cheese stick on top of the skewer. Wrap beef around the cheese and skewer, as tightly as possible. Repeat with remaining ingredients.

In a small bowl, combine all marinade ingredients. Arrange skewers side by side in a casserole dish and pour marinade over top. Let marinate in the refrigerator for at least 30 minutes.

Grill on the barbecue for 3 to 4 minutes over high heat, or on a baking sheet in a 450°F (230°C) oven for 5 minutes, turning halfway through. Serve.

KOREAN-STYLE BARBECUE PORK

12 SKEWERS

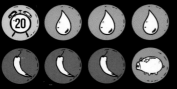

MARINATING TIME: 1 HOUR

12 slices pork belly (about 1/4 inch thick each), skin removed

FOR BARBECUE SAUCE

2 tbsp hoisin sauce
2 Thai chili peppers, finely chopped
2 tbsp homemade or store-bought barbecue sauce
2 tbsp soy sauce
2 green onions, thinly sliced
1 tbsp honey
1 tbsp lemongrass, grated

PREPARATION

In a bowl, combine all sauce ingredients. Add pork and mix well. Cover and let marinate in the refrigerator for at least 1 hour.

Thread meat onto pre-soaked wooden skewers.

Grill on the barbecue over high heat for 4 to 5 minutes, turning and brushing with sauce halfway through cooking. Serve with basmati rice or rice vermicelli.

FRUITY CHICKEN IN WHITE WINE

4 SKEWERS

MARINATING TIME: 2 HOURS

 TASTY TIP

If you want to barbecue these skewers instead, grill for 15 minutes over medium heat, and cook the sauce in a small pan. Just sauté a small, finely chopped shallot, deglaze with white wine, and finish with cream. Season with salt and pepper and serve!

 DID YOU KNOW?

The ancient Egyptians placed prunes, or dried plums, in tombs along with other provisions to feed the dead on their journey to the afterlife.

FOR SKEWERS

2 chicken breasts, cut into 1-inch cubes
8 dried apricots
8 pitted dried prunes
1/3 cup (80 ml) white wine
1/3 cup (80 ml) 35% cream
Salt and freshly ground pepper

FOR LEMON PARSLEY MARINADE

1 tsp cumin
Juice and zest of 1 lemon
1/4 cup (60 ml) fresh parsley, chopped
Salt and freshly ground pepper
1 tbsp sugar
1 shallot, halved
1/4 cup (60 ml) olive oil

PREPARATION

In a food processor, or with a hand blender, purée all marinade ingredients. In a bowl, combine chicken and marinade. Cover and let marinate in the refrigerator for at least 2 hours.

Preheat oven to 400°F (200°C).

Alternately thread apricots, chicken, and prunes onto pre-soaked wooden skewers.

Transfer to a casserole dish and cook in the oven for 10 minutes. Pour white wine and cream over all, season with salt and pepper, and cook for 10 minutes longer. Serve with sauce over a bed of couscous.

26

LAMB, CUMIN & DATES

4 SKEWERS

MARINATING TIME: 4 HOURS

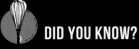

DID YOU KNOW?

In the Middle East, dates have been a staple food for thousands of years—in fact, archaeologists have discovered evidence of human consumption of the sweet fruit dating back 9,000 years!

FOR SKEWERS

1 lb (16 oz) lamb, cut into 1-inch cubes
2 cups (500 ml) eggplant, cut into 1-inch cubes
1 onion, cut into 1-inch pieces
1 zucchini, cut into 1/2-inch rounds

FOR CUMIN & DATE MARINADE

1 onion, roughly chopped
4 dates, pitted
1 tsp cumin
1/2 tsp ground ginger
1/2 tsp cinnamon
1/4 cup (60 ml) fresh cilantro
Juice and zest of 1 lemon
2 tbsp honey
2 tbsp vegetable oil
Salt and freshly ground pepper

PREPARATION

In a food processor, purée all marinade ingredients. Place lamb, eggplant, onion, and zucchini in a dish, add marinade, and mix well. Cover and let marinate in the refrigerator for at least 4 hours.

Alternately thread lamb and vegetables onto pre-soaked wooden skewers.

Grill over high heat on the barbecue, or in a grill pan with a ridged surface, for 8 to 12 minutes, turning halfway through cooking. Serve.

PORK & POTATOES, BASQUE STYLE

4 SKEWERS

FOR SKEWERS

12 new potatoes
1 pork loin, cut into 1-inch cubes
1 tbsp fresh thyme, chopped
2 tbsp olive oil
Salt and freshly ground pepper
1/4 cup (60 ml) fresh parsley, chopped

FOR BASQUE SAUCE

2 tbsp olive oil
1 red pepper, seeded and thinly sliced
1 onion, thinly sliced
2 tomatoes, quartered
2 cloves garlic, chopped
1/4 cup (60 ml) sherry vinegar
1/4 cup (60 ml) brown sugar
1 tsp celery seeds
Salt and freshly ground pepper

PREPARATION

In a small pot, cover potatoes with water and bring to a boil. Let simmer for 10 minutes, or until potatoes are easily pierced with a knife. Drain and set aside.

For Basque sauce: In a pot, heat olive oil and sauté pepper and onion for 5 to 6 minutes. Add tomatoes, garlic, vinegar, brown sugar, and celery seeds. Season with salt and pepper, cover, and let simmer for 20 minutes over low heat. With a hand blender, purée until smooth.

Cut potatoes in half. In a bowl, combine potatoes, pork, thyme, and olive oil. Season with salt and pepper. Alternately thread pork and potatoes onto pre-soaked wooden skewers.

Place skewers in an oven-safe dish and cook in a 450°F (230°C) oven for 10 minutes. Remove from the oven and pour Basque sauce over skewers. Lower oven temperature to 400°F (200°C) and cook for another 10 minutes. Sprinkle with parsley and serve.

TASTY TIP

Spice things up by adding 1 tsp crushed red pepper flakes or 1 tbsp piri-piri sauce to the Basque sauce!

28

SOY & ORANGE-GLAZED DUCK

4 SKEWERS

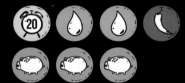

MARINATING TIME: 2 HOURS

 **TASTY TIP**

To perfectly cook these skewers in a grill pan with a ridged surface, just sear for 2 minutes on each side in a bit of oil, brushing frequently with marinade.

FOR SKEWERS

1 duck breast, cut into 12 cubes (about 1-1/2 inches x 1-1/2 inches each)
4 dried figs
1 leek, cut into 1/2-inch rounds

FOR SOY & ORANGE MARINADE

1/4 cup (60 ml) honey
2 tbsp soy sauce
2 tbsp rice vinegar
1 tsp ground coriander
2 tbsp fresh thyme, chopped
Juice and zest of 1 orange
2 cloves garlic, chopped

PREPARATION

In a bowl, combine all marinade ingredients. Add duck and figs and mix well. Let marinate in the refrigerator for at least 2 hours.

Alternately thread duck, figs (1 in the center of each skewer), and leek rounds onto pre-soaked wooden skewers. Brush with marinade and grill on the barbecue, or in a grill pan with a ridged surface, for 4 to 6 minutes, brushing with more marinade several times during cooking. Serve.

29

SWORDFISH, CILANTRO & LIME

4 SKEWERS

MARINATING TIME: 30 MINUTES

 **DID YOU KNOW?**

Swordfish are built for the hunt, and rely on swiftness and agility to catch their prey; their aerodynamic bodies and long bills allow them to reach incredible speeds.

1 lb (16 oz) fresh swordfish, cut into 1-1/2-inch cubes

FOR ORANGE & CILANTRO MARINADE

1 tbsp fish sauce
Juice of 1 lime
1/4 cup (60 ml) orange juice
1/4 cup (60 ml) white wine
4 drops Tabasco sauce
1/4 tsp freshly ground pepper
1 inch fresh ginger, peeled and chopped
1/4 cup (60 ml) fresh cilantro, chopped
2 green onions, thinly sliced

FOR TANGY PAPAYA SALAD

2 cups (500 ml) green papaya, peeled, seeded, and julienned
1/4 cup (60 ml) vegetable oil
1/4 cup (60 ml) rice vinegar
2 tbsp sesame seeds
1 cup (250 ml) vegetables of your choice (snow peas, carrots, etc.)
Salt and freshly ground pepper

PREPARATION

In a bowl, combine marinade ingredients. Add swordfish, cover, and let marinate in the refrigerator for at least 30 minutes, but no longer than 2 hours.

In a bowl, combine all papaya salad ingredients and let marinate in the refrigerator for at least 30 minutes.

Remove swordfish from marinade and thread onto pre-soaked wooden skewers. Reserve marinade.

Pour reserved marinade into a small pan and reduce until it turns into a syrupy sauce.

Grill skewers for 4 to 6 minutes over high heat on the barbecue, or in a grill pan with a ridged surface, turning halfway through cooking. Serve over papaya salad and drizzle with sauce.

TEX-MEX CHICKEN & GUAC

4 SKEWERS

FOR SKEWERS

4 chicken thighs, cut into 1-inch cubes
2 tbsp Dijon mustard
2 tbsp vegetable oil

FOR CAJUN COATING

1 tsp fresh thyme, chopped
1 tsp mild paprika
1 tsp brown sugar, packed
1 tsp cumin
1/2 tsp crushed red pepper flakes
1/2 tsp salt
1/4 cup (60 ml) breadcrumbs

FOR EXPRESS GUACAMOLE

1 ripe avocado
Juice of 1 lime
1/4 cup (60 ml) olive oil
Salt and freshly ground pepper

PREPARATION

In a small bowl, combine all Cajun coating ingredients.

Thread chicken onto pre-soaked wooden skewers and then brush with Dijon mustard. Spread Cajun coating on a large plate and roll the skewers in the coating.

Preheat oven to 350°F (175°C).

In a large pan, heat oil and sear skewers on all sides, until golden brown. Transfer to a baking sheet and cook in the oven for 10 minutes, or until chicken is cooked through.

With a hand blender, purée guacamole ingredients. Season with salt and pepper. Serve chicken with guacamole for dipping.

 **DID YOU KNOW?**

Tex-Mex cuisine is a fusion of Texan cooking and certain elements of Mexican cookery. Chili con carne, chimichangas, nachos, and fajitas are all Tex-Mex creations.

Historians have discovered that the Aztecs were making guacamole as early as the 16th century!

TRIPLE THREAT DESSERT BROCHETTES

4 SKEWERS

FOR SKEWERS

8 cubes homemade or store-bought brownies, 1 inch x 1 inch each
2 not-too-ripe bananas, cut into 4 pieces each
8 giant marshmallows

FOR CARAMEL SAUCE

2 tbsp butter
1/3 cup (80 ml) brown sugar
1/2 cup (125 ml) corn syrup
1 can (10 oz) sweetened condensed milk

PREPARATION

In a pot, combine butter, brown sugar, and corn syrup. Bring to a boil, stirring constantly. Reduce heat to medium and let simmer for 5 minutes. Remove from heat, add sweetened condensed milk, and stir with a wooden spoon until sauce is smooth.

Alternately thread 2 brownies, 2 banana pieces, and 2 marshmallows onto 4 pre-soaked wooden skewers.

Cook skewers for a few seconds over high heat on a well-oiled barbecue, or in an oiled grill pan with a ridged surface, just until the marshmallows are browned, but not melted.

Drizzle caramel sauce over skewers and serve.

TASTY TIPS

For the most decadent brownies you'll ever taste, try our recipe in *The World's 60 Best Desserts... Period.*

GOURMET GRILLED CHEESE SKEWERS

4 SKEWERS

INGREDIENTS

6 slices white bread
2 tbsp homemade or store-bought basil pesto
8 slices old Cheddar, Gruyere, or Manchego cheese
3 slices prosciutto or Serrano ham
2 tbsp homemade or store-bought sundried tomato pesto
1 tbsp butter

PREPARATION

On a flat work surface, lay out three slices of bread. Brush each slice with basil pesto and then top each with a slice of cheese, a slice of ham, and another slice of cheese. Brush remaining three slices of bread with sundried tomato pesto and close sandwiches.

Pile the three sandwiches on top of each other, placing a slice of cheese between each sandwich. Using a bread knife, cut off the crusts and then cut the sandwich tower into 4 mini towers. Pierce each mini sandwich tower with a skewer, threading all the way to the bottom.

In a pan, melt butter and cook sandwich skewers for 1 to 2 minutes on each side, until golden brown all over. Serve.

CHICKEN PARMESAN & MARINARA

6 SKEWERS

FOR CHICKEN PARMESAN

1/4 cup (60 ml) breadcrumbs
1/4 cup (60 ml) fresh Parmesan cheese, grated
2 tbsp fresh thyme, chopped
1 tsp mild paprika
Salt and freshly ground pepper
2 chicken breasts
2 tbsp flour
1 egg, beaten
Olive oil

FOR MARINARA SAUCE

1 tbsp olive oil
2 cloves garlic, chopped
1 cup (250 ml) canned crushed tomatoes
1 tsp sugar
Salt and freshly ground pepper
5 fresh basil leaves, chopped

PREPARATION

In a small bowl, combine breadcrumbs, Parmesan, thyme, and paprika. Season with salt and pepper and set aside.

Slice each chicken breast into 3 long strips. Thread onto pre-soaked wooden skewers, roll in flour, dip in egg, and then roll in breadcrumb mixture. Place in an oven-safe dish or on a baking sheet, drizzle with a bit of olive oil, and cook in a 375°F (190°C) oven for 20 minutes.

In a small pot, heat olive oil and sauté garlic. Add crushed tomatoes and sugar, and season with salt and pepper. Let simmer over low heat for 10 minutes, add basil, and remove from heat.

Serve skewers with hot or cold marinara sauce for dipping.

ORANGE GINGER SALMON & ASPARAGUS

12 SKEWERS

FOR SKEWERS

1 lb (16 oz) salmon, cut into 1-inch cubes
12 asparagus spears
1 tbsp olive oil
1 tbsp butter

FOR ORANGE GINGER GLAZE

1/4 cup (60 ml) orange marmalade
Juice of 1/2 lemon
1/2 tsp crushed red pepper flakes
1/2 inch fresh ginger, peeled and chopped
Salt and freshly ground pepper
1 tbsp fresh thyme, chopped

PREPARATION

With your hands, snap off the tough bottom ends of the asparagus stalks (they will break naturally where the spears become tender). Bring a large pot of water to a boil and blanch asparagus for 10 seconds. Immediately drain and plunge into cold water. Cut each asparagus into 3 equal pieces.

Alternately thread salmon and asparagus onto pre-soaked wooden skewers.

In a small bowl, combine all glaze ingredients. Brush salmon and asparagus generously with glaze.

In a large pan, heat olive oil and butter together over high heat. Sear skewers for 30 seconds on each side, and then pour remaining glaze into the pan. Rotate skewers to completely coat with sauce, remove from heat, and serve.

LEMONGRASS SHRIMP BALLS & PONZU

10 SKEWERS

FOR SHRIMP BALLS

1 tbsp lemongrass, grated
2 tbsp fresh chives, finely chopped
1 cup (250 ml) raw shrimp, peeled
1 inch fresh ginger, peeled and chopped
1/2 Thai chili pepper, seeded and chopped
1 tsp sesame oil
1 tbsp sesame seeds

FOR PONZU SAUCE

1/4 cup (60 ml) lemon juice
1/4 cup (60 ml) soy sauce
1/4 cup (60 ml) white wine
1 tbsp mirin

PREPARATION

In a food processor, very finely chop all shrimp ball ingredients, except sesame seeds. Cut lemongrass stalks into 4-inch lengths. Shape shrimp mixture into small balls and thread onto lemongrass stalks. Sprinkle with sesame seeds.

Transfer to a baking sheet lined with parchment paper and cook in a 350°F (175°C) oven for 20 minutes.

In a small bowl, combine lemon juice, soy sauce, white wine, and mirin. Serve skewers with ponzu sauce for dipping.

DID YOU KNOW?

The oil extracted from lemongrass stalks is commonly used as an insect repellent!

36

BEEF & MERGUEZ MEATBALLS

8 SKEWERS

INGREDIENTS

Meat from 2 merguez sausages
1/2 lb (8 oz) ground beef
1 red pepper, cut into 1-inch squares
1 tbsp vegetable oil
8 pickled pepperoncini peppers
8 pitted Kalamata olives

PREPARATION

In a bowl, combine sausage meat and ground beef. Shape into 1-inch meatballs.

Alternately thread meatballs and red peppers onto pre-soaked wooden skewers.

In a large non-stick pan, heat vegetable oil and cook meatballs for 10 to 15 minutes over medium heat, turning a few times during cooking.

Pierce 1 pepperoncini and 1 olive onto the end of each skewer and serve with pita bread and plain yogurt.

 DID YOU KNOW?

Merguez is a thin, spicy North African beef and lamb sausage, flavored with harissa, sumac, and cumin, with a characteristic bright red color.

THAI COCONUT CHICKEN

8 SKEWERS

MARINATING TIME: 4 HOURS

FOR SKEWERS

2 chicken breasts, cut into 1-1/2-inch cubes
1/2 cauliflower, cut into medium florets
18 cherry tomatoes

FOR THAI COCONUT MARINADE

1/3 cup (80 ml) coconut milk
2 tbsp fresh Thai basil, chopped
Juice and zest of 2 limes
1/2 tsp curry powder
1 clove garlic, chopped
1 onion, finely chopped
2 tbsp olive oil

PREPARATION

In a large bowl, combine marinade ingredients. Add chicken, mix well to coat, and let marinate in the refrigerator for at least 4 hours.

Alternately thread chicken and vegetables onto pre-soaked wooden skewers.

Grill on the barbecue over medium heat for 10 to 15 minutes, turning a few times during cooking. Serve with a squeeze of fresh lime juice and some fresh Thai basil.

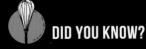

DID YOU KNOW?

An average coconut weighs between 16 and 24 oz, though one type of coconut from the Seychelles, the *coco de mer*, can weigh up to 776 oz!

38

SALMON CRÊPE ROLL-UPS

8 SKEWERS

FOR DILL CRÊPES

1 egg
1/2 cup (125 ml) milk
1 tsp sugar
1 pinch salt
1/2 cup (125 ml) flour
1 tbsp butter, melted
1/4 cup (60 ml) fresh dill, chopped

FOR SKEWERS

6 slices smoked salmon
1/4 cup (60 ml) cream cheese
8 pitted green olives
8 thin slices lemon

PREPARATION

In a bowl, whisk together egg, milk, sugar, and salt. Gradually sprinkle in flour, whisking constantly to prevent lumps from forming. Stir in melted butter and chill in the refrigerator for 15 minutes before making the crêpes. In a large non-stick pan over medium heat, cook 2 large crêpes, adding a bit of butter to the pan for each one. Set aside.

On a flat work surface, spread cream cheese onto crêpes and top each with 3 slices smoked salmon. Roll up into compact logs and slice into 1/2-inch rounds.

Thread an olive, a lemon slice, and 3 rounds onto each skewer. Serve on their own or with plain yogurt and roe.

39

BEEF & CHEDDAR BITES

8 SKEWERS

INGREDIENTS

1 onion, quartered
1/2 store-bought or homemade roasted red pepper
(see recipe on page 152)
2 cloves garlic
1/4 cup (60 ml) fresh parsley, chopped
1 tbsp Dijon mustard
1/2 cup (125 ml) cheddar cheese, grated
1 lb (16 oz) ground beef
1 egg
1/3 cup (80 ml) breadcrumbs
Salt and freshly ground pepper
Vegetable oil

PREPARATION

In a food processor, purée onion, roasted red pepper, garlic, parsley, mustard, and cheddar, until smooth.

In a large bowl, combine purée with ground beef, egg, and breadcrumbs. Season with salt and pepper and mix well, using your hands, to make sure the meat and cheese are blended. Shape mixture into meatballs and carefully thread onto pre-soaked wooden skewers.

Brush meatballs with vegetable oil and place on a baking sheet. Cook in a 400°F (200°C) oven for 10 to 15 minutes, turning skewers halfway through. Serve.

40

AL PASTOR PORK

4 SKEWERS

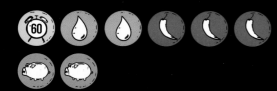

MARINATING TIME: 4 HOURS

DID YOU KNOW?

Al pastor is a variation on Middle Eastern *shawarma*, which was brought by Lebanese who immigrated to Mexico during World War I. Both are cooked on vertical rotisseries, but *al pastor* is typically made with pork marinated in dried chilis and cooked with pineapple, while *shawarma* is traditionally lamb-based.

Pineapple contains bromelain, a powerful enzyme that tenderizes meat by breaking down the proteins. If you're going to be cooking a tougher cut of meat, try a recipe with pineapple, nature's greatest tenderizer!

FOR SKEWERS

1 lb (16 oz) pork shoulder, cut into 1-inch cubes
2 cups (500 ml) fresh pineapple, cut into 1-inch cubes
1 red onion, cut into 1-inch cubes
1/2 cup (125 ml) fresh cilantro leaves
1 lime, cut into wedges

FOR AL PASTOR MARINADE

1 onion, quartered
1/2 cup (125 ml) orange juice
3 tbsp white wine vinegar
2 guajillo peppers, halved and seeded
2 cloves garlic
1 tbsp cumin

PREPARATION

With a hand blender, or in a food processor, purée onion, orange juice, white wine vinegar, guajillo peppers, garlic, and cumin. Transfer to a pan and let simmer on the stovetop over low heat for 15 minutes. Refrigerate. When marinade is cool, combine with cubed pork and pineapple, cover, and let marinate in the refrigerator for at least 4 hours.

Alternately thread pork, pineapple, and red onion onto pre-soaked wooden skewers.

Grill over high heat for 8 to 10 minutes on the barbecue, or in a grill pan with a ridged surface, turning a few times during cooking. Serve in tacos or over a bed of rice, garnished with fresh cilantro and lime wedges.

PORTUGUESE PIRI-PIRI CALAMARI

4 SKEWERS

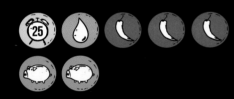

MARINATING TIME: 2 HOURS

FOR SKEWERS

1 lb (16 oz) small whole squids, skin removed, cleaned
1 lemon, cut into wedges

FOR PIRI-PIRI ORANGE MARINADE

1/4 cup (60 ml) Portuguese sweet red pepper paste (massa de pimentão)
1/4 cup (60 ml) white wine
Juice and zest of 1/2 orange
2 tbsp piri-piri sauce
4 cloves garlic, chopped
1 tbsp fresh thyme, chopped
1/4 cup (60 ml) fresh parsley, chopped

PREPARATION

In a bowl, combine all marinade ingredients. Add squid and mix well. Let marinate in the refrigerator for at least 2 hours.

Thread squid onto pre-soaked wooden skewers.

Grill on the barbecue over high heat for 4 to 6 minutes, turning halfway through cooking. Serve with a generous squeeze of lemon juice, and salad on the side.

 DID YOU KNOW?

The only parts of the squid that aren't eaten are its beak and its gladius, or pen, which is the hard internal shell that supports the squid's body, or mantle. The arms, tentacles, mantle, and ink are all edible.

42

CHICKEN YAKITORI

10 SKEWERS

MARINATING TIME: 1 HOUR

DID YOU KNOW?

Japanese *yakitori* is typically made with chicken, but in Japan, the word has come to designate any skewered food.

FOR YAKITORI MARINADE

1/2 cup (125 ml) soy sauce
1/4 cup (60 ml) mirin
1 clove garlic, chopped
1 inch fresh ginger, peeled and chopped

FOR CHICKEN MEATBALLS

2 chicken breasts, quartered
2 tbsp sake
1 egg white
1/4 cup (60 ml) flour

FOR SPICY MAYO DIP

1/4 cup (60 ml) mayonnaise or Kewpie (Japanese) mayonnaise
1 tbsp sriracha sauce
1 tsp rice vinegar

PREPARATION

In a small bowl, combine all marinade ingredients.

In a food processor, purée chicken, sake, and egg white until very smooth. Transfer to a bowl and add flour. Mix well, but don't season the mixture. With wet hands, shape into small, 1-inch meatballs. Transfer to a large bowl, coat with marinade, reserving 1/4 cup (60 ml) for later, and let marinate in the refrigerator for about 1 hour.

Thread 2 or 3 meatballs onto each of the pre-soaked wooden skewers.

In another bowl, combine all spicy mayo dip ingredients. Set aside.

In a large pan, heat 1 tbsp vegetable oil and cook chicken for 10 minutes over medium heat, turning halfway through cooking. Pour in 1/4 cup (60 ml) marinade 30 seconds before removing from heat to glaze the chicken. Serve with spicy mayo dip.

43

RETRO CANAPES

8 SKEWERS

MARINATING TIME: 2 HOURS

FOR QUICK-PICKLED VEGGIES

16 slices carrot, about 1/4 inch thick each
1 turnip, cut into 1/2-inch squares
8 pearl onions, peeled
16 slices Lebanese cucumber, about 1/2 inch thick each

FOR PICKLING BRINE

3/4 cup (180 ml) white wine vinegar
1/2 cup (125 ml) white wine
1 tbsp olive oil
1/4 cup (60 ml) sugar
1 tsp mustard seeds
1 tsp coriander seeds
1 tsp peppercorns

FOR SERVING

1/4 cup (60 ml) olive oil
1/2 baguette, cut into 1-inch slices
Salt
8 slices country pâté

PREPARATION

Bring a large pot of water to a boil and blanch carrot slices, turnip squares, and pearl onions for 3 minutes. Drain and let cool.

Alternately thread carrot slices, turnip squares, pearl onions, and cucumber slices onto small skewers and arrange, side-by-side and as tightly packed as possible, in a container or dish.

In a small pot, combine all brine ingredients. Bring to a boil, let simmer for 2 minutes, and pour over veggie skewers to cover them completely. Cover and let sit for 1 hour at room temperature, and then refrigerate for 1 hour longer, or until vegetables are cold.

Right before serving, heat olive oil in a pan and fry baguette slices a few at a time, for 1 to 2 minutes on each side, until golden brown. Season bread with salt and then top with pâté and vegetable skewers. Serve as a fun, '50s-inspired appetizer!

BACON, APPLE & CHICKEN

4 SKEWERS

FOR SKEWERS

1 chicken breast, cut into 1-inch cubes
1 apple, cut into 1-inch cubes
2 slices bacon, cut into 1-inch squares
4 chicken livers, cleaned and halved
Salt and freshly ground pepper

FOR BROWN SUGAR GLAZE

1 tbsp vegetable oil
3 tbsp brown sugar
2 tbsp soy sauce
1/2 inch fresh ginger, peeled and chopped
1 tbsp apple cider vinegar

PREPARATION

In a small pot, combine all glaze ingredients, stirring to make sure the brown sugar dissolves. Bring to a boil and let simmer for 5 to 8 minutes, until glaze is thick and syrupy. Set aside.

Alternately thread chicken, apple, bacon, and liver onto pre-soaked wooden skewers, making sure to start and finish with a piece of chicken. Season with salt and pepper.

Brush skewers with glaze and grill on the barbecue over medium heat for 10 minutes, turning a few times during cooking, and brushing with more glaze every 2 minutes. Brush with an extra coating of glaze right before serving.

MAPLE BACON-WRAPPED SHRIMP

4 SKEWERS

FOR SKEWERS

16 medium shrimp, peeled and deveined, tails left on
Salt and freshly ground pepper
8 slices bacon, cut in half
1 tbsp vegetable oil

FOR MAPLE GLAZE

1 tsp vegetable oil
2 tbsp pure maple syrup
2 tbsp sherry vinegar

PREPARATION

Season shrimp with salt and pepper and wrap each one with a half-slice of bacon.

Thread wrapped shrimp onto pre-soaked wooden skewers.

In a small bowl, combine maple glaze ingredients.

In a large non-stick pan, heat vegetable oil and cook skewers over high heat for 1 minute. After 1 minute, turn skewers and pour in maple glaze. Cook for 2 to 3 minutes longer, or until glaze is thick and coats the shrimp. Serve.

RACLETTE BROCHETTES

12 SKEWERS

INGREDIENTS

12 new potatoes
2 Toulouse sausages (or another mild sausage of your choice)
4 sprigs fresh rosemary
1 tsp salt
12 pearl onions, peeled
6 slices raclette cheese, cut in half

PREPARATION

Place potatoes, sausages, rosemary, and salt in a large pot, along with 8 cups of water. Bring to a boil, reduce heat to low, and let simmer for 10 minutes.

Remove sausages and then add pearl onions to the water. Let simmer for 5 minutes and then drain potatoes and onions. Let cool.

Cut potatoes in half. Slice sausages into 1/2-inch rounds. Alternately thread halved potatoes, sausage rounds, and onions onto 12 skewers.

Transfer skewers to an oiled oven-safe dish or pan and cook in a 400°F (200°F) oven for 5 minutes. After 5 minutes, top each with a half-slice of cheese and cook in the oven for 1 minute longer. Serve with gherkins (small, crunchy pickles).

 TASTY TIP

Because the traditional Swiss *raclette* meal is generally a relaxed, sociable affair, a fun alternative is to let your guests grill the skewers themselves over an electric table-top grill.

 DID YOU KNOW?

Raclette is actually a traditional Swiss dish. *Raclette* cheese is heated, scraped onto plates, and served with small potatoes, dried meat, gherkins, and pickled onions.

47

CHICKEN SATAY

8 TO 10 SKEWERS

MARINATING TIME: 2 HOURS

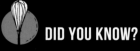

DID YOU KNOW?

Sate, or satay, is one of Indonesia's national dishes, and is sold at most eating establishments, from small street vendors to upper-class restaurants!

FOR SKEWERS

2 chicken breasts

FOR SATAY SAUCE

1/4 cup (60 ml) peanut butter
1/4 cup (60 ml) soy sauce
1/4 cup (60 ml) coconut milk
1 tbsp sriracha sauce
1/2 tsp curry powder
1 clove garlic, chopped

PREPARATION

Slice each chicken breast into 4 or 5 thin strips. Set aside.

In a bowl, whisk together peanut butter and soy sauce, until completely smooth. Whisk in coconut milk and then add sriracha, curry powder, and garlic. Keep whisking until sauce is well blended.

Put 1/4 cup (60 ml) of the sauce into a small bowl and refrigerate. Combine remaining sauce and chicken strips and toss to coat. Cover and let marinate in the refrigerator for at least 2 hours.

Thread chicken strips accordion-style onto pre-soaked wooden skewers.

Grill on the barbecue over medium heat for 6 to 8 minutes, turning halfway through cooking and brushing with sauce several times. Serve with reserved sauce for dipping.

48

SALMON STICKS & TARTAR SAUCE

10 SKEWERS

FOR SKEWERS

1 lb (16 oz) salmon, sliced into 3-inch strips
1/4 tsp cayenne pepper
Salt and freshly ground pepper
2 tbsp vegetable oil
1 tbsp butter

FOR TARTAR SAUCE

1/4 cup (60 ml) mayonnaise
2 tsp Dijon mustard
1 tsp honey
1 dill pickle, chopped
1 tbsp capers, chopped
2 sprigs fresh tarragon, leaves only, chopped
2 tbsp chervil or fresh parsley, chopped

PREPARATION

In a bowl, combine salmon strips and cayenne pepper, and season with salt and pepper. Mix well and thread onto pre-soaked wooden skewers. Set aside.

In a bowl, combine all tartar sauce ingredients.

In a large pan, heat oil and butter over high heat. Arrange salmon in the pan and cook until the underside is golden brown, about 1 minute. Remove pan from heat and flip skewers, allowing the salmon to finish cooking in the still-hot pan. Serve with tartar sauce.

MUCHO MUSTARD PORK SKEWERS

4 SKEWERS

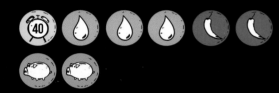

MARINATING TIME: 5 HOURS

FOR SKEWERS

1 lb (16 oz) pork shoulder, thinly sliced, and then cut into 1-1/2-inch squares
1/2 red onion, cut into squares
1/2 red pepper, cut into squares
1/4 cup (60 ml) white wine
1/3 cup (80 ml) 35% cream

FOR TWO-MUSTARD MARINADE

1 tbsp vegetable oil
2 tbsp piri-piri sauce
2 tbsp Dijon mustard
1 tbsp wholegrain mustard
1 tbsp fresh thyme, chopped
1/4 cup (60 ml) white wine

PREPARATION

In a bowl, combine all marinade ingredients. Add pork and mix well. Cover and let marinate in the refrigerator for at least 5 hours.

Alternately thread pork, onion, and red pepper onto pre-soaked wooden skewers.

Arrange skewers in an oven-safe dish and cook in a 450°F (230°C) for 10 minutes. Remove from oven and pour in white wine and cream. Stir, reduce heat to 400°F (200°C), and cook for another 10 minutes. Serve.

50

FUNKY FRUIT FONDUE

8 SKEWERS

FOR SKEWERS

24 red grapes
8 fresh raspberries
8 fresh strawberries
8 cubes cantaloupe, about 1-1/2 inches each
8 cubes pineapple, about 1-1/2 inches each
2 kiwis, peeled and cut into 4 rounds each

FOR CHOCOLATE SAUCE

1/2 cup (125 ml) 35% cream
1/4 cup (60 ml) milk
1/3 cup (80 ml) semi-sweet chocolate chips

PREPARATION

Assemble skewers by starting with three grapes, and threading the rest of the fruit in the order listed above (or any order you wish!).

To make the chocolate sauce, bring cream and milk to a boil in a pot. Pour mixture over chocolate in a bowl and whisk together until sauce is velvety.

Serve skewers with warm chocolate sauce for dipping.

VEAL ROMESCO ROULADES

4 SKEWERS

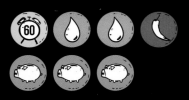

FOR SKEWERS

8 asparagus spears
1/4 cup (60 ml) goat cheese
4 veal cutlets

FOR ROMESCO SAUCE

1 store-bought or homemade roasted red pepper
(see recipe below)
10 hazelnuts
2 cloves garlic, sliced
1/4 cup (60 ml) olive oil
1 slice bread, toasted
2 tsp sherry vinegar
Salt and freshly ground pepper

PREPARATION

To roast the red pepper, rub the entire surface of a red pepper with 1 tsp vegetable oil and place on a baking sheet. Broil for 5 minutes on each side, or until skin is charred and easy to remove. Remove from oven, place in a bowl, and cover with plastic wrap. Let cool to room temperature. With your hands, split roasted red pepper and carefully remove seeds and skin.

In a pan, sauté hazelnuts and garlic in 1 tbsp of the olive oil, until lightly golden.

With a hand blender, or in a food processor, combine roasted red pepper, remaining olive oil, hazelnuts and garlic, bread, and vinegar. Season with salt and pepper and then purée until smooth. Set aside.

With your hands, snap off the tough bottom ends of the asparagus spears (they'll break naturally where the spears become tender). Cut spears in half. Bring a pot of salted water to a boil and blanch asparagus for 1 to 2 minutes, or until tender. Let cool.

Soften goat cheese in the microwave for a few seconds.

On a flat work surface, lay out veal cutlets, season with salt and pepper, and spread with goat cheese. Cut in half width-wise. Place 2 asparagus halves at the end of each veal piece and roll up as tightly as possible, around the asparagus. Slice each roll in half to make 16 rounds and thread onto pre-soaked wooden skewers. Cook over high heat for 3 to 4 minutes on each side, on the barbecue or in a grill pan with a ridged surface. Serve with romesco sauce.

LEMON SAFFRON SEAFOOD SKEWERS

4 SKEWERS

MARINATING TIME: 30 MINUTES

FOR SKEWERS

8 cubes halibut, about 1 inch each, skin removed
8 large scallops
8 shrimp, peeled and deveined
8 cherry tomatoes
1 red onion, cut into squares
1 zucchini, cut in half lengthwise and sliced into half-moons
1 tbsp olive oil
Salt and freshly ground pepper

FOR LEMON SAFFRON SEASONING

2 tbsp water
1 tsp saffron
1/2 tsp mild paprika
1 tbsp olive oil
Juice of 1/2 lemon
1 tsp cumin
1 onion, quartered

PREPARATION

To make the seasoning, heat the water and saffron for 30 seconds in the microwave, to allow it to infuse. In a food processor, combine with remaining seasoning ingredients.

In a bowl, combine seasoning, cubed halibut, and seafood, and mix well. Cover and let marinate for 30 minutes in the refrigerator.

In a bowl, combine vegetables and olive oil. Season with salt and pepper.

Alternately thread fish, seafood, and vegetables onto pre-soaked wooden skewers. Cook for 5 to 7 minutes on the barbecue, or in a grill pan with a ridged surface, turning half-way through cooking. Serve over a bed of baby spinach.

53

LAMB SOUVLAKI

4 SKEWERS

MARINATING TIME: 6 HOURS

 DID YOU KNOW?

Turkish *Doner Kebab* is made by stacking meat horizontally on a spit in the shape of an inverted cone and roasting it slowly on a vertical spit. The seasoned meat is sliced into very thin shavings and wrapped in a flatbread with vegetables and sauce. In Arabic, the dish is known as *shawarma*, and in Greek, as *gyro*.

FOR SKEWERS

1 lb (16 oz) lamb, cut into cubes
8 cherry tomatoes

FOR CLASSIC LAMB MARINADE

2 cloves garlic, chopped
2 tbsp fresh oregano, chopped
2 tbsp fresh mint, chopped
2 tsp crushed red pepper flakes
1 bay leaf
Juice and zest of 1 lemon
1/4 cup (60 ml) olive oil
1/4 cup (60 ml) white wine
Salt and freshly ground pepper

PREPARATION

In a large bowl, combine all marinade ingredients. Add cubed lamb, mix well, and cover and let marinate in the refrigerator for at least 6 hours.

Thread lamb onto pre-soaked wooden skewers, with a tomato at each end. Brush with marinade and grill for 6 to 8 minutes over high heat on the barbecue, turning a few times during cooking. Serve with pita bread and plain yogurt, or hummus.

SALTIMBOCCA SKEWERS

8 SKEWERS

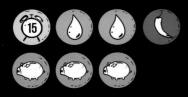

INGREDIENTS

4 veal cutlets
Freshly ground pepper
8 fresh sage leaves
4 slices prosciutto
2 tbsp butter
1/4 cup (60 ml) white wine
2 tbsp fresh Parmesan cheese, grated

PREPARATION

Lay out veal cutlets on a flat work surface. Season with pepper, and then top each cutlet with 2 sage leaves and 1 slice of prosciutto.

Slice each cutlet in half lengthwise, ensuring there is a sage leaf and some prosciutto on either side, and then thread accordion-style onto pre-soaked wooden skewers, making sure the ingredients are secure.

Place in a large oven-safe dish, prosciutto facing up, with 1 tbsp butter in the bottom of the dish. Cook in a 450°F (230°C) oven for 3 minutes. Remove from oven, add white wine and the rest of the butter, stir, and cook for another 2 minutes in the oven. Remove from oven, top with Parmesan, and roll skewers around in the butter to coat them all over. Serve.

 **DID YOU KNOW?**

Classic Italian *saltimbocca* (literally, "jumps in the mouth") is traditionally served rolled up and pierced with toothpicks.

HONEY GINGER PORK MEDALLIONS

4 SKEWERS

MARINATING TIME: 2 HOURS

FOR SKEWERS

1 pork loin
1 tbsp sesame seeds

FOR HONEY GINGER MARINADE

1/4 cup (60 ml) soy sauce
1/4 cup (60 ml) oyster sauce
2 tbsp ketchup
1/4 cup (60 ml) orange juice
1/4 cup (60 ml) honey
2 inches fresh ginger, peeled and finely chopped
1 onion, finely chopped

PREPARATION

Slice pork loin into medallions, about 1/2 inch thick each.

In a bowl, combine all marinade ingredients. Add pork medallions and mix well. Cover and let marinate in the refrigerator for at least 2 hours.

Thread medallions onto pre-soaked wooden skewers, using 2 skewers so the sides lie flat on the grill.

Grill over high heat for 10 minutes on the barbecue, or in a grill pan with a ridged surface, turning and brushing with more marinade halfway through cooking. Serve.

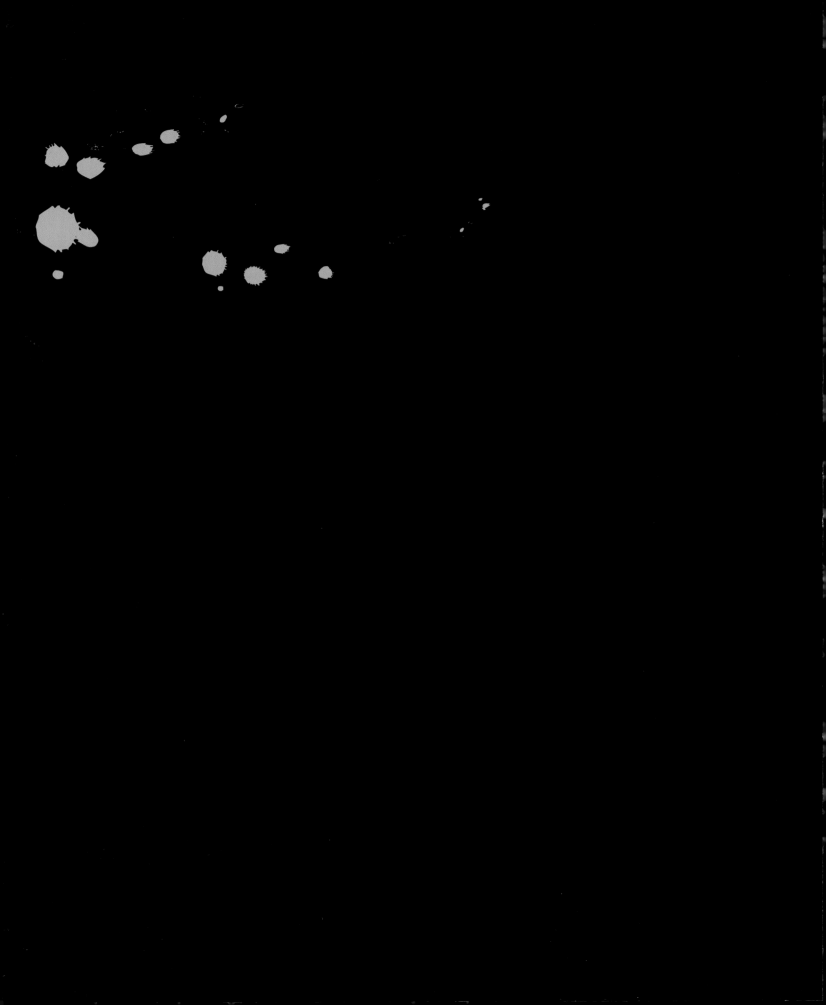

CRISPY SPICED SCALLOPS

4 SKEWERS

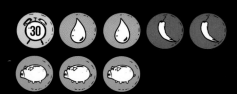

FOR SKEWERS

16 large or medium scallops
1 tbsp olive oil
1 tbsp butter

FOR SEAFOOD SEASONING

2 tsp fennel seeds
2 tsp dried dill
1/4 tsp crushed red pepper flakes
1 tbsp cornmeal
Zest of 1/2 lemon
2 tbsp fresh parsley
1/2 tsp sugar
1/2 tsp salt
1/4 tsp mild paprika
1/2 tsp freshly ground pepper

FOR LEMON CREAM SAUCE

Juice of 1 lemon
1/4 cup (60 ml) water
1/4 cup (60 ml) 35% cream
Salt and freshly ground pepper

PREPARATION

If necessary, remove the muscles from the scallops (the muscles are the little rectangular tags of tissue on the sides of the scallops) by pinching them and tearing them away, or slicing them off. Place scallops between two paper towels to sponge off any excess water.

With a mortar and pestle, grind fennel seeds, dill, and crushed red pepper flakes together. In a bowl, combine with remaining seasoning ingredients. Roll scallops in seasoning and thread onto pre-soaked wooden skewers.

In a large pan, heat olive oil, add butter, and sear skewers for 3 minutes on each side (2 minutes for medium scallops). Remove skewers from pan, deglaze pan with lemon juice, and add water and cream. Season with salt and pepper and cook sauce until it's thick enough to coat the back of a spoon. Serve skewers with sauce for dipping, or toss sauce with pasta and top with scallops.

CoCoNut CuRRY SHRiMP

4 SKEWERS

MARINATING TIME: 15 MINUTES

 **TASTY TIP**

Fresh cilantro has a lively, citrusy flavor that pairs perfectly with curry!

Make this your main course by adding lettuce and goat cheese to your mango salad.

FOR SKEWERS

12 medium shrimp, peeled and deveined, tails left on
1 tsp curry powder
1/2 tsp mild paprika
1 tbsp shredded unsweetened coconut
Juice of 1/2 lemon
1 tbsp vegetable oil

FOR MANGO SALAD

1 underripe mango, peeled
2 tbsp fresh chives, chopped
1/4 tsp ground ginger
1/4 tsp Espelette pepper
2 tbsp white wine vinegar
1/4 cup (60 ml) olive oil

PREPARATION

In a bowl, combine all skewer ingredients. Mix well, cover, and let marinate in the refrigerator for 15 minutes.

Using a cheese grater or a mandoline, finely grate or julienne the mango. In a bowl, combine mango with remaining salad ingredients. Refrigerate for 15 minutes.

Thread shrimp onto pre-soaked wooden skewers and grill over medium heat on the barbecue, or in a grill pan with a ridged surface, for 4 to 5 minutes, turning halfway through cooking. Serve over mango salad.

58

BEEF & BLUE CHEESE

4 SKEWERS

MARINATING TIME: 4 HOURS

TASTY TIP

Replace the shiitakes with your favorite wild mushrooms. Or take advantage of the intense, nutty flavor of succulent morels when they're in season!

FOR SKEWERS

1 lb (16 oz) beef, cut into 1-inch cubes
12 shiitake mushrooms, stems removed
1 red onion, cut into large cubes
Salt and freshly ground pepper
2 tbsp vegetable oil

FOR ROSEMARY MARINADE

1/3 cup (80 ml) vegetable oil
3 tbsp sherry vinegar
1 sprig fresh rosemary, leaves only
2 cloves garlic, thinly sliced
1 onion, finely chopped

FOR BLUE CHEESE SAUCE

1/4 cup (60 ml) white wine
1 cup (250 ml) store-bought demi-glace, prepared
1/4 cup (60 ml) 35% cream
2 tbsp blue cheese, crumbled
Salt and freshly ground pepper

PREPARATION

In a bowl, combine all marinade ingredients. Add cubed beef and mix well. Cover and let marinate in the refrigerator for at least 4 hours.

Alternately thread beef, mushrooms, and onion onto pre-soaked wooden skewers. Season with salt and pepper.

Preheat oven to 400°F (200°C).

In a pan, heat oil over high heat and sear beef until the exterior is browned on all sides. Transfer skewers to an oven-safe dish. Deglaze the cooking pan with white wine and add demi-glace, cream, and blue cheese. Season with salt and pepper and mix well. Pour sauce over skewers and cook in the oven for 6 to 10 minutes, until the beef has reached the desired doneness. Serve.

59

ASIAN-STYLE DELIGHTS

8 SKEWERS

MARINATING TIME: 1 HOUR

DID YOU KNOW?

The gizzard is an organ found in the digestive tract of birds, used for grinding up food. Ancient fossils suggest that dinosaurs also possessed gizzards!

Quail eggs are considered a delicacy in Western Europe and North America, but in other countries like Vietnam and the Philippines, they are a popular street food!

FOR SKEWERS

8 quail eggs
8 confit duck gizzards
2 green onions, cut into 4 lengths each
4 canned baby corns, halved
1 red pepper, cut into 1-inch squares
1 tbsp vegetable oil

FOR SOY-MIRIN MARINADE

1/2 cup (125 ml) soy sauce
1/4 cup (60 ml) mirin
1/4 cup (60 ml) brown sugar

PREPARATION

Bring a small pot of water to a boil. Carefully place eggs in the water and let simmer for 4 minutes. Drain, let cool, and peel.

Heat gizzards in the microwave for a few seconds to melt the surrounding fat.

In a bowl, combine all marinade ingredients. Add cooked quail eggs and gizzards, mix well, and let marinate in the refrigerator for at least 1 hour.

Thread a piece of each vegetable onto pre-soaked wooden skewers, finishing with a gizzard and an egg.

Cook in a 350°F (175°C) oven for 10 minutes, or on the top rack of the barbecue for 5 to 7 minutes. Serve.

SPICY CHICKEN & FETA TOMATO PESTO

6 SKEWERS

MARINATING TIME: 4 HOURS

2 chicken breasts, cut into 1-inch cubes

FOR SPICY KETCHUP MARINADE

1/4 cup (60 ml) ketchup
2 tbsp olive oil
2 tsp allspice
Salt and freshly ground pepper
1 onion, finely chopped

FOR FETA & TOMATO PESTO

1/4 cup (60 ml) fresh parsley
1/4 cup (60 ml) fresh cilantro
2 tbsp pine nuts
Juice of 1/2 lemon
1/4 cup (60 ml) olive oil
1/4 cup (60 ml) feta cheese, crumbled
1 Italian tomato, seeded and finely diced
Salt and freshly ground pepper

PREPARATION

In a food processor, purée all marinade ingredients. In a bowl, combine chicken and marinade. Cover and let marinate in the refrigerator for at least 4 hours.

Thread chicken onto pre-soaked wooden skewers.

Grill over medium heat for 10 to 12 minutes, on the barbecue, or in a grill pan with a ridged surface, turning a few times during cooking.

To make the pesto, purée parsley, cilantro, pine nuts, lemon juice, and olive oil in a food processor, until smooth. Transfer to a bowl and stir in feta and diced tomato. Season with salt and pepper and serve alongside skewers, or serve chicken and pesto in small pitas.

 **DID YOU KNOW?**

Allspice is the dried, unripened fruit of the *Pimenta dioica* tree. The small, red-brown, pea-sized berry tastes like a combination of clove, cinnamon, and nutmeg.

INGREDIENTS INDEX

MARINADES INDEX

SAUCES

SEASONINGS, GLAZES, SIDES, ETC.

CONVERSION CHART

1 dl	10 cl	100 ml
1 tablespoon		15 ml
1 teaspoon		5 ml
1 oz.		30 ml
1 cup		250 ml
4 cups		1 l
1/2 cup		125 ml
1/4 cup		60 ml
1/3 cup		80 ml
1 lb		450 g
2 lbs		900 g
2.2 lbs		1 kg
400°F	200°C	T/7
350°F	175°C	T/6
300°F	150°C	T/5

Volume Conversion
* Approximate values

---

1 cup (250 ml) crumbled cheese	150 g
1 cup (250 ml) all-purpose flour	115 g
1 cup (250 ml) white sugar	200 g
1 cup (250 ml) brown sugar	220 g
1 cup (250 ml) butter	230 g
1 cup (250 ml) oil	215 g
1 cup (250 ml) canned tomatoes	250 g

NOTES

....

....

....

....

....

....

....

....

....

....

....

....

....

....

....

....

....

....

....

....

60

IN THE SAME COLLECTION

THE WORLD'S **60** BEST
SALADS
PERIOD.

THE WORLD'S **60** BEST
BURGERS
PERIOD.

THE WORLD'S **60** BEST
LUNCHES
PERIOD.

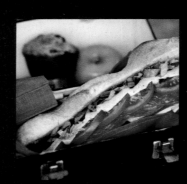

THE WORLD'S **60** BEST
RECIPES FOR STUDENTS
PERIOD.